WE'RE GONNA DIE

OTHER BOOKS BY YOUNG JEAN LEE
PUBLISHED BY TCG

The Shipment and *Lear*

Songs of the Dragons Flying to Heaven and Other Plays

ALSO INCLUDES:

Church
Pullman, WA
The Appeal
Groundwork of the Metaphysic of Morals
Yaggoo

WE'RE GONNA DIE

Young Jean Lee

THEATRE COMMUNICATIONS GROUP   NEW YORK   2015

We're Gonna Die is published by Theatre Communications Group, Inc., 520 Eighth Avenue, 24th Floor, New York, NY 10018-4156

The publication of *We're Gonna Die*, by Young Jean Lee, through TCG's Book Program, is made possible in part by the New York State Council on the Arts with the support of Governor Andrew Cuomo and the New York State Legislature.

TCG books are exclusively distributed to the book trade by Consortium Book Sales and Distribution.

LIBRARY OF CONGRESS CATALOGING-IN-PUBLICATION DATA
Lee, Young Jean.
We're gonna die / Young Jean Lee.—First edition.
pages ; cm
ISBN 978-1-55936-443-0 (softcover)
ISBN 978-1-55936-785-1 (ebook)
1. Death—Drama. I. Title. II. Title: We are going to die.
PS3612.E228W47   2015
812'.6—dc23   2015007280

Book design and composition by Lisa Govan
Book jacket designed by Benedict Kupstas
Cover art by Benedict Kupstas, inspired by a painting by Chad Wys

First Edition, June 2015

For Lou Reed

CONTENTS

WE'RE GONNA DIE

We're Gonna Die premiered in April 2011 at Joe's Pub in New York City. It was co-produced by 13P (Maria Goyanes, Executive Producer) and Young Jean Lee's Theater Company (Young Jean Lee, Artistic Director; Caleb Hammons, Producing Director). It was written by Young Jean Lee, directed by Paul Lazar and produced by Caleb Hammons. The choreography was by Faye Driscoll, the costume design was by Roxana Ramseur, the lighting design was by Cindy Shumsey; the sound engineer was Thanasis Psarros, the dramaturg was Mike Farry, the associate director was Morgan Gould, the production supervisor was Sunny Stapleton and the creative consultant was Eric Dyer. It was performed by:

Michael Hanf	DRUMMER
Nick Jenkins	BASS GUITARIST
Benedict Kupstas	GUITARIST 2
Young Jean Lee	SINGER
Tim Simmonds	GUITARIST 1

We're Gonna Die was developed in part through a residency at the National Theater Institute at the Eugene O'Neill Theater Center, and through the Lower Manhattan Cultural Council's Swing Space program (space at 14 Wall Street is donated by Capstone Equities), and was presented with support from the Andrew W. Mellon Foundation and the New York State Council on the Arts, a State Agency.

We're Gonna Die was remounted in September 2012 and again in August 2013 at LCT3's Claire Tow Theater (Paige Evans, Artistic Director) at Lincoln Center Theater in New York City. It was produced by Young Jean Lee's Theater Company (Young Jean Lee, Artistic Director; Aaron Rosenblum, Producing Director). It was written by Young Jean Lee, directed by Paul Lazar and produced by Aaron Rosenblum. The choreography was by Faye Driscoll, the costume design was by Roxana Ramseur, the lighting design was by Tyler Micoleau; the sound designer was Jamie McElhinney, the dramaturg was Mike Farry, the associate director was Morgan Gould and the production supervisor was Sunny Stapleton. It was performed by:

Michael Hanf	GUITARIST I
Andrew Hoepfner	BASS GUITARIST
Benedict Kupstas	GUITARIST 2
Young Jean Lee	SINGER
Booker Stardrum	DRUMMER

All of the stories in this show are true, but not all of them happened to me, so although I originally performed the piece, the character of "Singer" is not meant to be me. Instead, the show is designed for anyone to be able to perform as themselves without adopting a theatrical persona. For that reason, performers should feel free to make whatever small changes are necessary in order to make the text feel natural for them to perform.

The band should be good, with real musicians who have interesting takes on the songs. Once they enter, they remain onstage for the rest of the show. During the monologues, they watch and listen in stillness. In the original production, the arrangements grew more full and more complex, song-by-song, over the course of the show.

A stage is set up with instruments and microphones on stands.

There is upbeat pre-show indie pop music.

An Announcer, wearing ordinary street clothes, enters and goes to one of the microphones.

The Announcer introduces the piece and warms up the crowd without mentioning any of the performers' names or creating any expectation that a star is about to take the stage. In the original production, we used the following text. Whatever speech you come up with, it should end like the announcement below, with the words: "And now: We're Gonna Die.*"*

ANNOUNCER
Good [afternoon/evening] and welcome to [name of venue]. I'm [name], the [job title] of [name of company/theater/venue]. *We're Gonna Die* was originally written for 13P, which was a collective of thirteen playwrights who were devoted to realizing full productions of each of their plays. Now that they have done all thirteen plays,

13P has imploded. This was number eleven. Please turn off your cell phones. And now: *We're Gonna Die.*

(The Announcer exits as the Singer enters holding a cordless microphone. She wears yellow jeans, a blue sweater with a sailboat on it, and sneakers. She smiles at the audience.)

SINGER

When I was growing up, my mother would always try to scare my sister and me by saying, "You'd better behave, or you're gonna end up like your Uncle John." And this was actually a pretty effective threat, because my Uncle John is the most isolated person I've ever known. He's always lived alone; he doesn't have a single friend; as far as anyone knows, he's still a virgin; and for as long as I can remember, he's spent every major holiday with my family.

And it's this awful paradox because, on the one hand, we all feel really terrible for my Uncle John and for how lonely he is. But at the same time, none of us really wants to be around him either. He smells bad, he's rude, and whenever he comes to visit, he just kind of sits there and lets everyone wait on him.

And he's always had this weirdly lethargic quality. I remember when I was growing up, I would always ask him, "Uncle John, do you want to play with me?" And he would always respond, "Why don't we just sit here and rest?"

So when I was twelve, I decided that I wanted to see what my Uncle John was like in a more animated state. So one night, when he went to brush his teeth before going to sleep, I snuck into his room and I hid under his bed. And my plan was that when he went to get into bed, I was going to grab his ankles and give him a little surprise.

So I'm under my Uncle John's bed, waiting for him to come back from brushing his teeth. But when he came back into the room, instead of going right to bed, he went and sat down at a little desk that was in the room, and I heard him start to mutter something to himself. He was muttering it over and over, and at first I couldn't understand what he was saying, but then he started to get louder and louder.

And I heard that what he was saying was, "I'm a piece of shit, piece of shit, piece of shit, I'm shit, I'm shit, I'm shit," over and over again. And then he started to cry.

And I was under his bed!

Obviously, I couldn't do the ankle-grabbing thing anymore, so I just started panicking, like I didn't know how much longer I was going to be stuck under there. And all the while, my Uncle John is like, "I'm a piece of shit, piece of shit," and crying. Until, suddenly, he stopped.

And then I heard a loud snore. He had fallen asleep at his desk. And as I got the hell out of there, I remember wondering to myself if this was how my Uncle John fell asleep every night.

Looking back on that story now, the thing that strikes me the most is the fact that even my Uncle John, weird Uncle John, had a public face that he put on to cover up the true extent of his suffering. When you're little, it's sort of more okay to cry and freak out when you're upset, but the older you get, the more necessary it becomes to develop this public face that you put on to hide your pain. And it's not even like you can rip off the mask and let it all hang out

11

when you're in private around people who care about you, because there's only so long you can go on dumping your pain on other people before they eventually start to get fed up. Which can make being in pain an incredibly lonely experience.

This is something that has always really bothered me a lot, and I've always wished that there were some form of comfort available to us so that, when we were in that isolated place of pain, there would be something to make us feel better and not so alone. And I always imagined that if I found that comfort, it would take the form of something big and revelatory and amazing. But when I have encountered actual comfort in my life, it's never been anything like that. It's usually been something really ordinary and common sense.

For example, there's this thing that my mom said to me when I was six and experiencing that awful, alone, in-pain feeling for the very first time. At the time, I had two best friends named Emily and Jenny. They were sisters who lived across the street. My favorite memory of Emily and Jenny is this one time when they came over and their grandparents had bought them bicycles. Neither of our families had any money, so this was like a huge deal. And I didn't have a bicycle, so I remember running alongside them as they rode their bikes until eventually they would overtake me, and then I would walk back home and wait for them to come back so that I could run alongside again. And I did this over and over again, until eventually Emily turned to me and said, "Hey, why don't we teach you how to ride a bike so that you can take a turn?" And I was so excited.

But it turns out that learning how to ride a bike from six year olds is not the best idea. I was bleeding from every joint, and I couldn't go inside and get cleaned up because if my mom had seen me, she would have freaked out and made me stop, and at this point all I wanted out of life was to be able to ride a bicycle. So I kept at it, becoming increasingly injured, until eventually I got to the point where I could do it—I could ride the bike.

Emily had volunteered to be the one to chase after, and she saw me covered in blood, and she got inspired. And she said, "Why don't we pretend that I'm an advertising executive?" (For some reason, Emily always wanted to be an advertising executive. I don't think she even knew what it was.) But she said, "I'm an advertising executive, and you have just murdered my husband. And that's why you're covered in blood. And now you are trying to escape on your bicycles."

So Jenny and I rode off down the street with Emily chasing us screaming, "Murderers! You murdered my husband!" And Jenny and I were like, "Ha ha ha! You'll never see your husband again!"

And we called that game Murder, and we played it all the time after that.

About a year later, a new girl moved into the neighborhood, and her name was Mary Didio. And she started to play with us, and eventually it got to the point where she was playing with Emily and Jenny and I wasn't invited. And then finally one day at school during recess, the three of them were playing together, and I walked up to them, and they all kind of looked at each other, and then Emily said, "One! Two! Three! GO!" And the three of them just ran away from me as fast as they could. And it was really clear that I was not supposed to chase them.

I remember going to the nurse's office and telling her that I had a stomachache, and she let me lie down on a little cot that she had in her office. And then I started to cry, so she thought I was really sick and called my mother to come pick me up.

(The Band enters wearing brightly colored shirts. They start lightly playing their instruments to underscore the following.)

That night, as I was lying in bed, for the first time in my life I experienced the feeling of not being able to fall asleep. And I had this tiny little attic bedroom with these two little windows right above my bed, and I remember staring at the branches through the windows for a really long time. And eventually my mom came in to check on me, and I told her that I couldn't sleep, and this is what she said to me.

LULLABY FOR THE MISERABLE

In the dead of the night
With your eyes open wide
You will sleep
By and by
By and by

All alone in the dark
With the pain in your heart
You will sleep
By and by
By and by

When you wait for the dawn
And sleep won't come

If you don't sleep tonight
It's all right, it's all right
You will sleep
By and by
By and by

(Instrumental Break)

When all your hope is gone
. And sleep won't come

When your brain's had enough
And your body gives up
You will sleep
By and by
By and by

Fast asleep in your bed
Not a thought in your head
You will sleep
By and by
By and by

You are not the only one
You are not the only one
You are not the only one
You are not the only one

So that's the kind of thing I'm talking about. Like I said, it's not some big profound thing, but I feel like it's better than nothing. And that's the type of thing I'd like to share with you tonight: just some sort of ordinary comforting things that have somehow managed to make me feel a little better when I was in that lonely, isolated place. And I'm sharing them with you in the hopes that they might help you to feel less lonely when you're in pain—which I hope you're not.

Okay, so a lot of people believe that the best way to not feel alone is to find romance. But, as most of you know, there are a lot of problems with that—one of the biggest ones being that not everyone can find it. I didn't find romance until I had graduated from college. When I was in high school, I didn't date at all. And then when I was in college, I dated a series of alcoholics, none of whom were my boyfriend, which I knew because they would all tell me, "You're not my girlfriend."

But then I graduated from college, and I sort of started to get my life together, and I met this amazing guy named Henry. Henry was smart, he was funny, and he was really nice to me. And after we'd been dating for about a year, we moved in together.

And it was around that time that my parents decided to host this big family reunion at their house. And I was really excited because I'd always kind of been the black sheep of the family—I had an older sister who had always been very successful and popular. And yet even she had never brought home a guy as wonderful as Henry. So I was really eager to go home and show him off.

So we went to the reunion, and everyone was *really* impressed by Henry, like almost to an offensive extent? I was like, "Is it really that amazing that I managed to find a good boyfriend?"

But it was great, and I remember all the cousins were playing softball in the backyard the way we used to when we were kids. And the ball rolled into the bushes by the kitchen door, and I went to go look for it. And the kitchen door was open, and my mom was in the kitchen with one of my aunts. And I heard my mom tell my aunt that she could never feel the same way about me as she felt about my sister.

That night, I told Henry what had happened, and he was really nice about it, but he was an only child, so he didn't really understand, and then he fell asleep. And as I was lying there, this is what I thought to myself.

I STILL HAVE YOU

When life deals me a blow
And I'm reeling in pain
You try to comfort me
But it doesn't go away

You tell me that you love me
Before you fall asleep
And as I lie awake
With my worries on repeat

I try to think of something
That can ease my grief
And the answer comes right to me
While I listen to you breathe

I still have you
You're in my bed
You'll hold my hand
Until I'm dead

If you die first
I'll be alone
But until then
I'll have a home

Last night I had a dream
That I'd lost my mind
I woke up in a panic
Of overwhelming fright

I realized how close we are
To madness and despair
The truth of my own weakness
Was more than I could bear

But then I saw you next to me
When I turned on the light
I reached for you
And in your sleep you held me tight

I still have you
You're in my bed
You'll hold my hand
Until I'm dead

If you die first
I'll be alone
But until then
I'll have a home

Today you were so miserable
And anxious all day long
It's been that kind of week
Where everything goes wrong

You don't deserve the things
That have been happening to you
I wanna make them go away
But what can I do?

I try to cheer you up
But I can't fix anything
Life is what it is
All I can do is sing

You still have me
I'm in your bed
I'll hold your hand
Until you're dead

If I die first
You'll be alone
But until then
You'll have a home
You'll have a home

So of course, a year later Henry dumped me. It was one of those awful things where you sense the person pulling away, so you cling on even more desperately, and it goes on for way too long, and it's horrible, and eventually he had to pull the plug.

On the day that he moved out, I told him that I couldn't stand to see him move out all his things, so I was going to a friend's house. But before I left, I made him promise that he would rearrange all of the furniture before he left so that there wouldn't be these big gaps where all of his things used to be, because it would just be too painful for me to have to walk in and see that. So Henry promised that he would do this for me, and I went to my friend's house. When I came back later that night, I opened the door and saw that Henry had rearranged everything perfectly—he had even dusted so that there weren't any marks where any of his things used to be.

The only problem was that he had had this giant wide-screen television that had been the focal point of our living room, and obviously he had taken it with him because it was his. And on this big table where the television used to be, he had put a doily and two candlesticks.

And I saw that and just burst into tears. And I ran into the bedroom and saw that half the books were missing from the shelves. And that's when it hit me: now I live here alone.

COMFORT FOR THE LONELY

The only words of comfort for the lonely
The very words that they will never hear
The only words of comfort for the lonely
The very words that they will never hear

(Instrumental Break)

The only words of comfort for the lonely
The very words that they will never hear
The only words of comfort for the lonely
The very words that they will never hear

(Instrumental Break)

I'm coming over now
I'm coming over now
I'm coming over now
I'll be right there

(Instrumental Break)

I'm coming over now
I'm coming over now
I'm coming over now
I'll be right there

I'm coming over now
I'm coming over now

I'm coming over now
I'll be right there
I'll be right there

About a year ago, I went back home for a younger cousin's wedding, and while I was at home, I found my first white hair. Now, I had never been a person who worried at all about getting older or losing my looks—I just never thought about that stuff. So it all just kind of hit me in this one moment, and I had this major overreaction.

I realized that if my whole life had been an upward climb through learning how to walk and talk and read and get better at things and stronger, that I had reached the point in my life where everything from here on out was going to be a downward decline towards deterioration and sickness and death. And this had never occurred to me before, so I was really traumatized.

I remember going into my mother's bedroom and showing her the white hair, and I told her that I was freaking out. And she told me a story about something her grandmother once said to her. So, in this next song, I'm gonna be doing my first and only impersonation of the evening, and it's gonna be a double impersonation: I'll be doing an impersonation of my mother's impersonation of her grandmother.

WHEN YOU GET OLD

My mother's mother lived to be a hundred
She died when I was just a little child
Before she passed she called me to her deathbed
She pulled me close, and this is what she said,

"When you get old
You will lose your mind!
And everything will hurt all the time!
Uh-huh
Uh-huh"

I cried and started calling for my mother
My mother's mother gripped me with her claw
She said, "Be quiet child and stop your fussing
There's something more:

When you get old
All your friends will die!
And you will be a burden to the world!
Uh-huh
Uh-huh"

(Instrumental Break)

My mother's mother held me to her bosom
She smoothed my hair and spoke into my ear,
"Getting old has been for me a blessing
Now I face death with little fear

If we got old
And we were strong and healthy
We wouldn't wanna die!
Oh no!

If we got old
And didn't feel like dying
We wouldn't wanna go!
Uh-huh
Uh-huh
Uh-huh
Uh-huh"

My father was a very healthy person. He ate healthy, he exercised, he never smoked a day in his life. And when he turned sixty, he was diagnosed with advanced stage lung cancer and told that he had a year and a half left to live. Because he was so healthy, he managed to survive chemo for three years. He worked the whole time, he never complained, he was amazing.

So one day, my dad goes to the doctor, and the doctor says that there's a clinical trial for a new miracle drug for lung cancer patients. And this drug is so crazily effective that, in some people, they see a shrinkage in their cancer the very next day after taking the drug. The only catch is that the drug is only effective in the less than two percent of the population that have this really rare genetic mutation. But if you're one of those two percent, the drug can save your life.

The clinic where the trial was being held was about a six-hour drive from where my parents lived, and my father wasn't in great shape to travel, but they made the trip, and he went through two days of intensive testing to see if he had the genetic mutation. And after he did the tests, they came back home and waited for a month for the results. And they were kind of worried the whole time that even if the results came back positive and my father was eligible, that he'd be too sick to make the trip back to the clinic for the trial.

But finally, the phone call came and, unbelievably, my dad was one of the two percent—he had the genetic mutation. And he was just well enough to travel. So my parents made the trip back to the clinic, and when they got there, the nurse looked really upset. And she said, "I'm sorry, but there's been a mistake."

And my parents started freaking out, and she said, "No, no, you have the genetic mutation—you're totally eligible for the trial. The only problem is that one of the blood samples we took was too small. So unless we retake the sample and wait another month for the results, we're not gonna be able to use your results in the trial, and therefore cannot release the medication." My parents asked to speak to the doctor, and they explained to him that they couldn't wait a month because my father probably wouldn't live that long, so could he please just give them the medication to save my father's life. And the doctor felt really bad and said, "I wish I could, but I'd lose my license. But what I can do is try to put a rush on the blood sample, and hopefully it will come back sooner than a month and you'll be able to take the medication."

So my parents checked into a hotel and waited. And while they were there, my father's condition continued to decline to the point where he couldn't breathe at all lying on his back, not even with an oxygen tank. So he would sit awake all night struggling to breathe, and eventually it got so bad that he had to go to the hospital and get a tube put down his throat so that he could breathe.

And that was the day that I showed up. My family was exhausted, so I took over for them at the hospital, and I remember my father was communicating by writing on a pad. And we worked out this system of hand signals that he would use to communicate with me so that I could tell the nurses what he wanted.

That night, I was sleeping on a cot in his hospital room, and suddenly all the alarms started going off, the lights came on, the nurses came running into the room. And I got up and saw my father sitting upright in the bed. His arms were tied to the bed, and he just had this look on his face of such terror. Like, I have never seen a more horrible expression. It reminded me of something out of one of those Renaissance paintings of Hell. And he was just freaking out, and he was doing everything in his power to get that tube out of his throat. And it took three nurses and me to restrain him so that they could sedate him again.

After that happened, I turned to the nurses and said, "What the hell was that?" My father was the calmest person, he would just never do that. And the nurses explained to me that sometimes when you give patients sedation, when they wake up, they have no idea who they are or where they are. All they know is that they're strapped to this scary bed with this horrible thing going down their throat, and they panic. And she said, "Don't worry, it's totally normal."

So this happened like five or six times over the course of the night, and I was getting so mad at the nurses. I was like, "Just give him enough sedation so that he doesn't wake up and this doesn't keep happening to him!" And they felt terrible and said, "We wish we could, but if we give him that much, we'll kill him. We're trying to do this very delicate balancing act."

And then an even more horrible thought occurred to me, which was: what if it's not even the case that he doesn't know who he is? What if he is conscious, and he's trying desperately to communicate something, and that's why he wants the tube out of his throat? So I told this to the nurses, and they said, "Even if that's the case, if we take the tube out, he'll die. So there's really nothing we can do." And this kept going on all night.

The next morning, the blood sample came back confirming my father as eligible for the trial. And that afternoon, he died.

After this happened, I was so enraged. Just the perversity of that sequence of events. And my father was such a good person, and for him to die that way, and for me to see it. I just couldn't get over it, and I wasn't eating, I couldn't sleep at all. If I did manage to fall asleep, I would have horrible nightmares and wake up with this feeling of dread that I was going to die exactly the way my father did. And if anyone tried to help me, I would just get angrier and angrier, and nobody could do anything. Until I got a letter from my friend Beth.

But before I tell you what Beth's letter said, I have to tell you a little about Beth.

When my friend Beth was about to turn forty, she had been married for twelve years to a really charming and successful guy, and they had two beautiful children, ages three and six. And they were all in the car on their way back from a weekend family outing. My friend Beth was driving, her husband was in the passenger seat, and the two kids were in the back. And Beth's husband's cell phone was on the divider between them.

The phone rang, and Beth looked down and saw that it was one of his co-workers, Anita. And he rejected the call. And Beth asked, "Oh, why didn't you take that call from Anita? If she's calling on a weekend, it must be something important about work." And he just gave her some answer that didn't make any sense at all.

And Beth thought that was strange, and it sort of continued to bother her all day. And that night, she was lying awake at two in the morning, and it was still bothering her, this phone call. So she wakes up her husband and says, "Look, I know something was weird with that phone call today. You tell me right now what it is."

And he gets up, and says, "Okay, I've been trying to figure out how to tell you this. I guess now is the time."

Basically, for the past twelve years of their marriage, plus the four years they'd been dating before that, this man had been sleeping with strippers, prostitutes, random women he'd picked up in bars. He said it was like over a hundred women. And the first words that came out of Beth's mouth were, "Did you use condoms?" And he said, "Not usually. But, but! You were always the one who I loved. Those other women were just sex. I always loved you."

Until Anita, this woman from work. They'd been seeing each other for the past six months, they were in love, and now Anita wanted to have a baby. So Beth's husband was going to leave my friend Beth and their kids for this woman, Anita.

Obviously, it's the night from hell. My friend Beth doesn't get any sleep. And the next morning, she's in the shower and, in a total freak accident, she somehow manages to slip and fall, and, in the process of falling, claws out her own cornea.

(Light musical underscoring begins.)

True story.

So after this happened, I was one of the people who helped Beth through the trauma of that experience. And since then, she had moved across the country. And when she heard about what had happened to my father, she wrote me a letter, and this is what the letter said.

HORRIBLE THINGS

It's horrible what happened
And I'm sorry that you're suffering
You probably won't feel better for a while

Don't worry I won't tell you
To get on with your life
And I promise I won't try to make you smile

I don't know what you're going through
But I know what it's like to want to die
When life insists on going on

That's when I sing a little song
That makes me feel a little better

Just a little
Not a lot

Who do you think you are?
To be immune from tragedy?
What makes you special?
That you should go unscathed?

(Instrumental Break)

It's horrible what happened
And I'm sorry that your mind is filled
With all those agonizing memories

I regret that I
Can't help with words of comfort
Or reassuring expertise

But I know what it's like to cry
How could this have happened?
Why on earth should I be cursed?

That's when I sing a little song
That makes me feel a little better
Just a little
Not a lot

Who do you think you are?
To be immune from tragedy?
What makes you special?
That you should go unscathed?

(Instrumental Break)

Horrible things happen all the time
Horrible things happen all the time

So after I read Beth's letter, I asked myself, "Okay, so, who do you think you are?" And the answer was, "I think I'm special." I believe, deep down, with all my heart, that I deserve to be immune not only from loneliness and tragedy, but also from aging, sickness and death.

(Light musical underscoring begins.)

But I'm not special. I'm a person. And when you're a person, all kinds of really terrible things can happen to you. That's why my father died the way he did, and if I die the same way, it'll be for the same reason: because I'm a person. Just like my father, just like my Uncle John, just like everyone. And again, it wasn't some big, profound revelation. But, for the first time in a long time, I felt a very little bit of comfort.

I'M GONNA DIE

I'm gonna die
I'm gonna die someday
Then I'll be gone
And it'll be okay

I'm gonna die
I'm gonna die someday

Then I'll be gone
And it'll be okay

(Instrumental Break)

I'm gonna die
I'm gonna die someday
Then I'll be gone
And it'll be okay

I'm gonna die
I'm gonna die someday
Then I'll be gone
And it'll be okay

Someone will miss me
Someone will be so sad
And it'll hurt
It's gonna hurt so bad

Someone will miss me
Someone will be so sad
And it'll hurt
It's gonna hurt so bad

(Instrumental Break)

I'm gonna die
I'm gonna die someday
Then I'll be gone
And it'll be okay

I'm gonna die
I'm gonna die someday
Then I'll be gone
And it'll be okay

Someone will miss me
Someone will be so sad
And it'll hurt
It's gonna hurt so bad

Someone will miss me
Someone will be so sad
And it'll hurt
It's gonna hurt so bad

(Instrumental Break)

We're alive but we can't live forever
We can't keep each other safe from harm
We're alive but we can't live forever
We can't keep each other safe from harm

We're alive but we can't live forever
We can't keep each other safe from harm
We're alive but we can't live forever
We can't keep each other safe from harm

We're gonna die
We're gonna die
We're gonna die
We're gonna die

We're gonna die
We're gonna die
We're gonna die
We're gonna die

*(Singer starts singing "We are going to die" in counterpoint to the
rest of the Band)*

BAND	SINGER
We're gonna die	We are going to die
We're gonna die	
We're gonna die	
We're gonna die	
We're gonna die	We are going to die
We're gonna die	
We're gonna die	
We're gonna die	
We're gonna die	We are going to die
We're gonna die	
We're gonna die	
We're gonna die	
We're gonna die	We are going to die
We're gonna die	
We're gonna die	
We're gonna die	
	We are going to die

(As the Band finishes playing "We're Gonna Die," a dance remix track of the song fades up.

Drummer hits his cymbal and the others whip their heads to look at him and start rocking back and forth with the beat.

Drummer jumps up on his stool and does a solo dance with his drumsticks.

As Drummer continues to dance on the stool, Guitarist 2 and Guitarist 1 dance in place with their guitars while Singer and Bass Guitarist do a synchronized, floppy-handed, bunny-hop-like dance.

When they finish, Guitarist 1 and Guitarist 2 stride toward each other and embrace in a bear hug. They spin together and then separate while still holding their arms in the shape of the hug.

Guitarist 1 does an awkward solo dance, squatting and moving his knees like scissors while waving his hands wildly. He finishes with a spin and twists his arms like a flamenco dancer over his head as he looks out at the audience.

Drummer, flapping his arms in a swan-like manner, is carried on Bass Guitarist's shoulders from his stool to the downstage area, where Guitarist 1 helps him down.

Singer and Guitarist 2 shake their butts in unison stage right and stage left, respectively, while Bass Guitarist and Drummer do a dance where they squat down in unison while Guitarist 1 pops up from behind them.

Everyone gets into a formation with Guitarist 1 in the center, and Singer and Guitarist 2 pumping their outside arms and legs on either side.

Singer and Guitarist 2 dive through Drummer and Bass Guitarist's legs, respectively, then pop out between Drummer, Guitarist 1, and Bass Guitarist's torsos for an instant before retreating back behind them.

Everyone spins around Guitarist 1 to create a five-person water-skiing pose.

Then, Guitarist 2 and Bass Guitarist make a human swing with their arms for Drummer, who swings back and forth in their arms like a kid on a swing set.

Meanwhile, Singer and Guitarist 1 hop to center with their arms outstretched in presentational diagonals. Singer and Guitarist 1 squat and shuffle in a tight circle around each other, while Guitarist 2, Bass Guitarist, and Drummer back them up with side-to-side clapping.

Everyone claps their way into a symmetrical formation and suddenly breaks into a synchronized dance of head turns and angular arm motions that ends with everyone holding hands in a line and rocking back and forth.

Guitarist 2, Bass Guitarist, Guitarist 1, and Drummer create a body-builder formation while Singer does push-ups off Bass Guitarist and Drummer's knees, smiling at the audience.

Singer hops forward and everyone faces the audience in a line. The dance music fades out as everyone begins to sing an a cappella version of "We're Gonna Die.")

A CAPELLA I'M GONNA DIE

I'm gonna die
I'm gonna die someday
Then I'll be gone
And it'll be okay

I'm gonna die
I'm gonna die someday

Then I'll be gone
And it'll be okay

Someone will miss me
Someone will be so sad
And it'll hurt
It's gonna hurt so bad

Someone will miss me
Someone will be so sad
And it'll hurt
It's gonna hurt so bad

We're alive but we can't live forever
We can't keep each other safe from harm
We're alive but we can't live forever
We can't keep each other safe from harm

We're alive but we can't live forever
We can't keep each other safe from harm
We're alive but we can't live forever
We can't keep each other safe from harm

We're gonna die
We're gonna die
We're gonna die
We're gonna die

(Singer starts singing "We are going to die" in counterpoint to the rest of the Band)

BAND	SINGER
We're gonna die	We are going to die
We're gonna die	
We're gonna die	
We're gonna die	

(Singer encourages the audience to sing "We are going to die" in counterpoint to the melody sung by the Band)

	(Speaking:)
	Everybody!
	(Back to singing:)
We're gonna die	We are going to die
We're gonna die	
We're gonna die	
We're gonna die	

	(Speaking:)
	I can't hear you!
	(Back to singing:)
We're gonna die	We are going to die
We're gonna die	
We're gonna die	
We're gonna die	

	(Speaking:)
	Good job!
	(Back to singing:)
We're gonna die	We are gonna die

BAND   SINGER
We're gonna die
We're gonna die
We're gonna die

(Speaking:)
Woo!
(Back to singing:)
We're gonna die   We are going to die
We're gonna die
We're gonna die
We're gonna die

(Speaking:)
One more time!
(Back to singing:)
We are going to die   We are going to die

(Blackout.)

END OF PLAY

CHORD SHEETS

LULLABY FOR THE MISERABLE

    F#   C#
In the dead of the night
         F#   B
With your eyes open wide
         F#
You will sleep
         C#
By and by
        B   F#
By and by

    F#   C#
All alone in the dark
         F#   B
With the pain in your heart
         F#
You will sleep
         C#
By and by
        B   F#
By and by

    G#m   B   F#
When you wait for the dawn
      G#m   C# G#m C#
And sleep won't come

    F#   C#
If you don't sleep tonight
      F#   B
It's all right, it's all right
      F#
You will sleep
      C#
By and by
      B   F#
By and by

Instrumental Break
F# C# F# B F# C# B F#

      G#m   B   F#
When all your hope is gone
      G#m   C#   G#m C#
And sleep won't come

       F#   C#
When your brain's had enough
      F#   B
And your body gives up
      F#
You will sleep

```
      C#
By and by
      B          F#
By and by


      F#         C#
Fast asleep in your bed
      F#            B
Not a thought in your head
      F#
You will sleep
      C#
By and by
      B          F#
By and by


F#      G#m  C#    F#
You are not the only one
D#m     G#m  C#    F#
You are not the only one
F#      G#m  C#    F#
You are not the only one
D#m     G#m  C#
You are not the only one
```

Coda
F# B F# B F# B F# B

I STILL HAVE YOU

F#
When life deals me a blow
And I'm reeling in pain
B
You try to comfort me
      F#
But it doesn't go away

F#
You tell me that you love me
  G#m   C#
Before you fall asleep
    D#m
And as I lie awake
       B
With my worries on repeat

  E
I try to think of something
       A
That can ease my grief
       B
And the answer comes right to me
       C#
While I listen to you breathe

I STILL HAVE YOU

     F#
I still have you
        B
You're in my bed
          F#
You'll hold my hand
      C#
Until I'm dead

     F#
If you die first
  B
I'll be alone
    F#
But until then
    C#
I'll have a home

F#
Last night I had a dream
That I'd lost my mind
  B
I woke up in a panic
  F#
Of overwhelming fright

   F#
I realized how close we are
    G#m   C#
To madness and despair
    D#m
The truth of my own weakness
     B
Was more than I could bear

   E
But then I saw you next to me
      A
When I turned on the light
  B
I reached for you
             C#
And in your sleep you held me tight

       F#
I still have you
         B
You're in my bed
          F#
You'll hold my hand
       C#
Until I'm dead

             F#
If you die first
         B
I'll be alone
             F#
But until then
              C#
I'll have a home

       F#
Today you were so miserable
And anxious all day long
       B
It's been that kind of week
                   F#
Where everything goes wrong

       F#
You don't deserve the things
                  G#m   C#
That have been happening to you
    D#m
I wanna make them go away
        B
But what can I do?

    E
I try to cheer you up
       A
But I can't fix anything
B
Life is what it is
     C#
All I can do is sing

        F#
You still have me
       B
I'm in your bed
       F#
I'll hold your hand
      C#
Until you're dead

    F#
If I die first
     B
You'll be alone
     F#
But until then
      C#
You'll have a home
      F#
You'll have a home

COMFORT FOR THE LONELY

Bm	D	G	A	Bm	D	E	F#m

The only words of comfort for the lonely

Bm	D	G	A	Bm	D	E	F#m

The very words that they will never hear

Bm	D	G	A	Bm	D	E	F#m

The only words of comfort for the lonely

Bm	D	G	A	Bm	D	E	F#m

The very words that they will never hear

Instrumental Break
A

Bm	D	G	A	Bm	D	E	F#m

The only words of comfort for the lonely

Bm	D	G	A	Bm	D	E	F#m

The very words that they will never hear

Bm	D	G	A	Bm	D	E	F#m

The only words of comfort for the lonely

Bm	D	G	A	Bm	D	E	F#m

The very words that they will never hear

Instrumental Break
A

```
        D           A        G
I'm coming over now
        D           A        G
I'm coming over now
        D           A        G
I'm coming over now
          D         A        G
I'll be right there
```

Instrumental Break
```
Bm        D         G        A      Bm      D      E,     F#m
Bm        D         G        A      Bm      D      E      F#m
A
```

```
        D           A        G
I'm coming over now
        D           A        G
I'm coming over now
        D           A        G
I'm coming over now
          D         A        G
I'll be right there
```

```
        D           A        G
I'm coming over now
        D           A        G
I'm coming over now
```

      D   A   G
I'm coming over now
          D   A   G
I'll be right there
         D
I'll be right there

Coda
D   Em   F#m   G
Bm   A   D   Em

WHEN YOU GET OLD

Instrumental Theme
A F#m

    A
My mother's mother lived to be a hundred
   Bm   D
She died when I was just a little child
  G   D
Before she passed she called me to her deathbed
              A
She pulled me close, and this is what she said,

Bm   F#m
"When you get old
C#   D
You will lose your mind!
    G   D
And everything will hurt all the time!
A   F#m
Uh-huh
A   F#m
Uh-huh"

   A
I cried and started calling for my mother
      Bm   D
My mother's mother gripped me with her claw

<pre>
    G   D
She said, "Be quiet child and stop your fussing
                      A
There's something more:
</pre>

<pre>
Bm   F#m
When you get old
C#   D
All your friends will die!
      G   D
And you will be a burden to the world!
A   F#m
Uh-huh
A   F#m
Uh-huh"
</pre>

Instrumental Break
F#m A F#m A
G D A
F#m A F#m A
G D

<pre>
      A
My mother's mother held me to her bosom
      D
She smoothed my hair and spoke into my ear,
</pre>

D/A   D/B
"Getting old has been for me a blessing
        A
Now I face death with little fear

Bm   F#m
If we got old
    C#   D
And we were strong and healthy
    G   D
We wouldn't wanna die!
    A
Oh no!

Bm   F#m
If we got old
     C#   D
And didn't feel like dying
     G   D
We wouldn't wanna go!
A   F#m
Uh-huh
A   F#m
Uh-huh
A   F#m
Uh-huh
A   F#m
Uh-huh"

HORRIBLE THINGS

Intro
A F#m E
A F#m E
E A B

    E
It's horrible what happened
And I'm sorry that you're suffering
    A   B
You probably won't feel better for a while

    E
Don't worry I won't tell you
To get on with your life
    A   B
And I promise I won't try to make you smile

    E
I don't know what you're going through
                                  A
But I know what it's like to want to die
                       B
When life insists on going on

        E
That's when I sing a little song
That makes me feel a little better
      C#m
Just a little
    A
Not a lot

           E
Who do you think you are?
  B   A
To be immune from tragedy?
          E
What makes you special?
        B   A
That you should go unscathed?

Instrumental Break
EM7

    E
It's horrible what happened
And I'm sorry that your mind is filled
    A   B
With all those agonizing memories

E
I regret that I
Can't help with words of comfort
A   B
Or reassuring expertise

E
But I know what it's like to cry
How could this have happened?
       A   B
Why on earth should I be cursed?

            E
That's when I sing a little song
That makes me feel a little better
     C#m
Just a little
    A   Am
Not a lot

           E
Who do you think you are?
   B   A
To be immune from tragedy?
            E
What makes you special?
         B   A
That you should go unscathed?

Instrumental Break
A F#m E
A F#m E

E   A C   E
Horrible things happen all the time
E   A C   E
Horrible things happen all the time

I'M GONNA DIE

     B
I'm gonna die
I'm gonna die someday
     D
Then I'll be gone
   B
And it'll be okay

     B
I'm gonna die
I'm gonna die someday
     D
Then I'll be gone
   B
And it'll be okay

Instrumental Break

     B
I'm gonna die
I'm gonna die someday
     D
Then I'll be gone
   B
And it'll be okay

       B
I'm gonna die
I'm gonna die someday
        D
Then I'll be gone
      B
And it'll be okay

        B
Someone will miss me
Someone will be so sad
      E
And it'll hurt
      B
It's gonna hurt so bad

        B
Someone will miss me
Someone will be so sad
      E
And it'll hurt
      B
It's gonna hurt so bad

Instrumental Break

      B
I'm gonna die
I'm gonna die someday
       D
Then I'll be gone
    B
And it'll be okay

      B
I'm gonna die
I'm gonna die someday
       D
Then I'll be gone
    B
And it'll be okay

      B
Someone will miss me
Someone will be so sad
     E
And it'll hurt
     B
It's gonna hurt so bad

        B
Someone will miss me
Someone will be so sad
       E
And it'll hurt
        B
It's gonna hurt so bad

Instrumental Break
B D B

B   D
We're alive but we can't live forever
       A   B
We can't keep each other safe from harm
B   D
We're alive but we can't live forever
       A   B
We can't keep each other safe from harm

B   D
We're alive but we can't live forever
       A   B
We can't keep each other safe from harm
B   D
We're alive but we can't live forever
       A   B
We can't keep each other safe from harm

B
We're gonna die
We're gonna die
   D
We're gonna die
   B
We're gonna die

B
We're gonna die
We're gonna die
   D
We're gonna die
   B
We're gonna die

Singer starts singing "We are going to die" in counterpoint to the rest of the Band

BAND	SINGER
We're gonna die	We are going to die
We're gonna die	
We're gonna die	
We're gonna die	
We're gonna die	We are going to die
We're gonna die	
We're gonna die	
We're gonna die	

I'M GONNA DIE

BAND	SINGER
We're gonna die	We are going to die
We're gonna die	
We're gonna die	
We're gonna die	
We're gonna die	We are going to die
We're gonna die	
We're gonna die	
We're gonna die	
We are gonna die	We are going to die

YOUNG JEAN LEE is a writer, director, and filmmaker who has been called "the most adventurous downtown playwright of her generation" by the *New York Times* and "one of the best experimental playwrights in America" by *Time Out New York*. She has written and directed ten shows in New York with Young Jean Lee's Theater Company, and toured her work to more than thirty cities around the world. Her plays have been published by Theatre Communications Group (*Songs of the Dragons Flying to Heaven and Other Plays*, *The Shipment* and *Lear*, and *We're Gonna Die*) and Samuel French (*Three Plays*). Her first short film, *Here Come the Girls*, was presented at the Locarno International Film Festival, Sundance Film Festival, and BAMcinemaFest. In 2013, she released her debut album, *We're Gonna Die*, with her band Future Wife. Lee is the recipient of a Guggenheim Fellowship, two Obie Awards, a Prize in Literature from the American Academy of Arts and Letters, a Doris Duke Performing Artist Award, a Doris Duke Artist Residency, a Foundation for Contemporary Arts grant, and the ZKB Patronage Prize of the Zürcher Theater Spektakel. She has also received funding from the National Endowment for the Arts, the New York State Council on the Arts, the Rockefeller MAP Fund, the Andrew W. Mellon Foundation, Creative Capital, the Greenwall Foundation, the Jerome Foundation, the New York Foundation for the Arts, the Arts Presenters/Ford Foundation Creative Capacity Grant, the Barbara Bell Cumming Foundation, and the New England Foundation for the Arts: National Theater Project Award.

ALBUM CREDITS

TRACK LISTING

Monologues and SONGS

1. Uncle John (read by Adam Horovitz)
2. Emily & Jenny (read by Kathleen Hanna)
3. LULLABY FOR THE MISERABLE
   (Featuring Sarah Neufeld)
4. Family Reunion (read by Sarah Neufeld)
5. I STILL HAVE YOU
6. Henry (read by Martin Schmidt)
7. NO COMFORT FOR THE LONELY
   (Featuring Colin Stetson)
8. White Hair (read by Drew Daniel)
9. WHEN YOU GET OLD
10. Father (read by David Byrne)
11. Beth (read by Laurie Anderson)
12. HORRIBLE THINGS
13. Conclusion (read by Colin Stetson)
14. I'M GONNA DIE

Future Wife is Michael Hanf, Andrew Hoepfner, Nicholas M. Jenkins, Benedict Kupstas, and Young Jean Lee. Monologues and lyrics by Young Jean Lee. Music by Young Jean Lee and Tim Simmonds, except: "When You Get Old" by Young Jean Lee, Tim Simmonds, and Benedict Kupstas; "No Comfort for the Lonely" by Young Jean Lee, Tim Simmonds, Benedict Kupstas,

ALBUM CREDITS

and Future Wife. Monologuists: Laurie Anderson, David Byrne, Drew Daniel, Kathleen Hanna, Adam Horovitz, Sarah Neufeld, Martin Schmidt, and Colin Stetson. Additional musicians: Shannon Fields (various instruments on all songs), Sarah Neufeld (violin on "Lullaby for the Miserable"), and Colin Stetson (saxophones on "No Comfort for the Lonely").

Produced by Shannon Fields at The Run-In (Jordanville, NY) and The Isokon (Woodstock, NY). Recorded, engineered, and mixed by D. James Goodwin at The Isokon. Vocals on "Horrible Things" recorded by Shannon Fields and Jonathan Kreinik at Midnight Sun (Brooklyn, NY). Additional instrumental overdubs recorded by Shannon Fields at The Run-In. Mastered by Nathan James at The Vault (New York, NY). Arrangements by Future Wife, Tim Simmonds, and Shannon Fields. String arrangements on "Lullaby for the Miserable" by Sarah Neufeld. Saxophone arrangements on "No Comfort for the Lonely" by Colin Stetson.

A project of Young Jean Lee's Theater Company (Aaron Rosenblum, Producer).

Infinite gratitude: 13P, Laurie Anderson, David Byrne, Aurélie Charon, Bart Cortright, William Cusick, Evan "Funk" Davies, Doris Duke Charitable Foundation, Faye Driscoll, Eric Dyer, Paige Evans and all at LCT3, Mike Farry, Kate Gagnon, Morgan Gould, Caleb Hammons, Kathleen Hanna, Adam Horovitz, Jeff Janisheski and all at the O'Neill, Rachel Karp, Yuri Kwon, Paul Lazar and Big Dance Theater, Inn-Soo Lee, Jason Lee, Lower Manhattan Cultural Council, Lubov, TaraFawn Marek, Matmos, Nello McDaniel, Sarah Neufeld, Antje Oegel, Park Avenue Armory, Roxana Ramseur, Lou Reed, Aaron Rosenblum, Tim Simmonds, Sunny Stapleton, Booker Stardrum, Colin Stetson, Shanta Thake and all at Joe's Pub, Virtual Label, Blake Zidell and Associates, John Zorn and all at the Stone, and all our families and friends.